Hiccups

Hiccups

or, Autobiomythography II

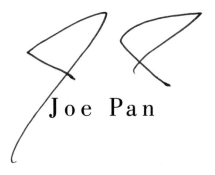

Joe Pan

Augury Books
New York, New York

Hiccups
© 2015 Joe Pan

ISBN-13: 978-0-9887355-4-5

Cover design by David Drummond

First Edition

Second Printing

Contents

for Wendy

Last day of spring always
our first day—becoming lobsters,
we regenerate

The dewdrop world
is just a dewdrop world
& yet— & yet—

—Issa

Atlas

I-95

Big rigs sashay
        across broken lines
to the windshield wipers' aria

Florida

    Pinesap popping
    in the brush fire—
    ash our simple snow

    Sticky vinyl seats
    reek of suntan lotion
    & all light the same color!

New York City

Laptop on a park bench—
man watches a movie
of people in a park

Washington Square Park—
Pilot Glasses mates The Moustache—
A king falls beneath the pigeon's glare

Workaday dawn. Two women
recognize each other revolving
through revolving doors

Man caught in the subway doors;
sometimes changing your mind hurts

Advertisement on faded brick—
park squirrel grooms its belly—
Bill Murray recites lines over tea—
weaving cars somehow miss a jaywalker—
some days are about sitting still

Consciousness
Leaf suspended
between passing
subway cars

With the whole underground
          rattling in womb,
she balances, two fingers on a pole

Nights at the advertising firm—
quartered moon over the Empire
State Building, unbranded

A spider
        needles through a bonsai
                sixteen stories above 42nd St

Noon moon—
        city sidewalk—
gyro sauce dripping from aluminum

Rockabilly bebop on Ave B—
Lakeside Lounge opens to honor
roll rejects, platinum blonds—
I'm forgetting to do something

Top of the skyscraper—
woman who's afraid of heights
wears a skirt that isn't

Brooklyn

Old Polish women pass
linked sausages between them—
long checkout line

In the curl of her ear
a whisper I can't manage
from across the platform

Auditioning elastic sex
the artist strips to a car alarm—
the stage lights clap off

Belly to bar at the Soft Spot—
dusty in rouge smoke, clipped laughter—
rap meth in Portland, Park Slope
as the new Midwest

Grease fire on the boardwalk—
child's stubbed & bloodied toenail—
Hell is Coney Island

Subdued Brooklyn light splayed
over red-orange dental dog brick—
words fail to exhaust the natural world

Long Island City—music pulsing
over water—man in cat ears
prowls the beach club

Beacon

Extra wine bottle after the opening—
old wiseass tippler, hated art, loved our booze,
passed through by a passing car yesterday…

Vermont

She loads the wood at dawn—
fire stoked at dusk under a water
barrel collecting us, snowflakes

Farmdogging chickens a swarm
of feathered fish—evening arrives
a lonely hippopotamus

Boston

Even luck
has standards
poker punk

Harvard
Quo Vadis Structural Biology?—
radish-faced academic points the way
with a laser the color of a radish

DC

Green shoots on one side
of a January branch—
half choose hope

Congress—the mighty chambers—
a heart? a stomach?—two dogs
wrestling over street meat

Bowling for Silver Spring
Ten tall thin pins or ten short stout pins?
Having arrived from a traffic jam outside
a hostage crisis, this unimpeachable need
to anticipate any skirting of widths—

Pecos River, Texas

My hand upon a man's hand
blown red with paint dust
ten thousand years ago

<u>Petroglyphs</u>
Constellations cut in black
rock beneath my feet
as we wobble through space

Walking our canoe in tall grasses
alongside the river rush I hear
a taxi slam into a dump truck

Monument to nothing,
the river's white stone monolith
a tendon between blues

The South

Crawfish, a hundred perhaps, boiling
in a pot—a lava of spooning hoards—
we'll suck the juices from their heads
& sex ourselves to sleep.

The Midwest

Chipping away
the storefront lettering,
an apothecary becomes a pharmacy

Hass in Iowa
Interrupting our class with silence
to identify a bird by its vocalizations—
you asked why dead people stay that way

Chicago

Conference writers huddle
the publisher's table—
which are the jackals?

Big Sky Country

Cruising the dark plains
at top speed—yellow-green eyes
hitchhike my low-gas fear

Yellowstone
The earth gargles
its thousand throats—
this bear has indigestion

The Southwest

Bluegray truck carries
wind to the sunset—
desert green

Zions
Mesa wind, snow crunched
underfoot—resistance
is how we come to know desire

Ant lost
among monolithic snails—
Bryce Canyon at dusk

Horse between my legs
carries the extra weight
of breakfast on his mind

Canyon snow—
if there is a point to all this,
the hoodoos aren't talking

Canyon walls
& my horse dressed
in the same rough color

Desert moon
inhabits the empty frame
of mind

Mule I straddle gazes
into the Grand Canyon & pisses—
I know how you feel

Vegas

One drink, two
drinks, three drinks,
floor

At the pai gow table
losing money, I'm told
I speak "normal, like TV"

MGM Grand
Lion in the hotel
puts on a show
of being a lion

$6,321,496.00 jackpot—
my quarters sure pay
for a lot of pretty lights

Desert moon
just another bulb
in Vegas

Los Angeles

Bel Air mansion courtyard—
you & me, hummingbird,
& neither dressed appropriately!

Diamondbacks vs Angels—
hot dogs in a summer hail—
back-seat sex our holy materialism

Pier, surfer, rock jetty—
three nouns
under the same cold light

Venice Beach—
lollipop wrappers
in full bloom

Midnight harmonica
on the beach, even
the fire can't sit still

San Diego

<u>With Gary at St Vincent de Paul Village</u>
The homeless wait
outside, inside, around
the corner, within

Long-legged pink flamingo
flies into my lap—the zoo, the boy bar

San Francisco

LucasArts
Yoda sits atop the fountain—
atop he is not, being the fountain—
the fountain he is not, being Yoda

Portland

Eyes shut, head to the speaker,
the trucker's daughter erases
magazines & moldy trades, her cash
register, my annoying voice—

Gay pride parade—
& on the prowl,
a pride

<u>Mary's</u>
"Partyboob" is booby trap spelled
backwards. Strap-on is "no parts."
The pole dancer laughs upside down,
lights her cigarette comically.

Seattle

Lemon-infused air,
melon-infused salmon—
the waitress' ear, that cusp of hair

Pacific Northwest

Log cabin—
bugs practice shadow puppets
behind the green leaf

As if it's nothing,
black ant stands sideways
on a log, takes a bow

Mt. Rainier National Forest—
live 1000 years & they honor you
with a bench made from yourself

Over many springs
these trees have changed their minds
on how the rocks should look

Listening for birds, I hear the river—
listening for the river, I hear birds

Haystack Rock
A dizzy halo of maritime birds
have led a mountain astray
& onto the tongue of an ocean

The campfire spits,
turns away & exhales—
best to let it cool off

Nestled in ocean rocks
a starfish
points us home

The smell of cedar rising
in a forest of ancient patriarchs—
even my mind whispers

Chipmunk stops, looks about
& leans in—mushroom
bends to listen

Glacial blue waters rub raw
a Douglas fir testing the temperature
with a toe branch before slowly wading in

Juneau

Valley of waterfalls—
Iditarod huskies howl
in chorused anticipation
of the trace chain

Anchorage

Black table hardened with indeterminate crust—
soiled, foam-sheathed barstool cut & upchucking its insides—
a sad, lived-in silence—scent of a plucked orange blossom,
far from home—to some we'd be worth more as oil

The Bay

This glacier knows
how to build a valley
but lacks confidence

```
                h
        t       t
        s       u
        a       o
     N E W S   from a Decade
     o       e
     r       s
     t       t
     h
```

North
Inclement weather
& another fallen star
finds God

East
New wind carries
smoke from a car
bomb into the terminal

West
The governor who killed
robots for a living
laughs like a robot

South/New Orleans
Thousands led to a stadium's
mouth—the stadium
is fed better

Tokyo

The art & toys of a generation
mushroom from a fat boy—
huge infant eyes, plastic grin

<u>Vintage</u>
Dear former shirt-wearer—
I have taken what was 'yours'
to Tokyo—she breathes better here

'Authentic Japanese' cuisine in fancy hotel
poisons me—
azalea blossoms in a swirling Charybdis

Girl in an anime costume
animates the animal mojo of my
animus—Harajuku hentai

Early morning May rain—
Shinjuku skyscrapers
slip on their cellophane jackets

Cherry blossoms, as iris blossoms
in the pupil, blossom in the iris—
beat on, heart, beat on

On opposite sides of Chuo-dori
oppositional protesters
berate each other with bullhorns

Glazed-over look of pond carp
as they nip the dark surface—
every bar with a mirror

Rush-hour commuters
speedwalk the plaza—crow feathers
lengthening a stream

China

A wall of bones & stone
uproots the countryside—
watchtower for the winter mind

<u>Returning from 798 Art Zone</u>
Empty cities rise
from nothing, for nothing,
through smog for no one,
      for no one, climb, for never

Taiwan

Drunken god dances before
the temple fire—shark eyes
floating in a bucket

South Africa

The sea split the land
with a river & some people
still haven't forgiven it

Window, electric fence—
what separates lions
from an international breakfast

Elephant trunk slips about a low
bough's trigger—pulls
back—sparks of birds erupt

The difference between
cheetah & the idea of cheetah
is my hand on its head, this purr

O ornamented kingfisher—
as if the green hills were made
to accommodate such ego

The lioness wakes, yawns,
stretches her nails into the dirt
& the bowels of my fear

The pathos of the day
divided into the hacked
millimeters of a rhino horn

Cutout switchback hills—a whiplash
of cold rain—muddy pockmarks juggle
the truck tires—my virus on adventure

Canoe stuck in the bottom-sucking
riverbank muck forces us out—
blue-balled vervets cackling like bastards

The activist cuts leopard bait
from the blesbok's rough hide
as maggots eat out a circle of praise

In this heat
the kind of animal you are
emerges on the slopes

Barcelona

The ghost of Gaudí
still peering through the rose
ribcage of a stillborn

Seville

Thrashed bed sheets—
you wake blue from sex, palms
wet as palms drowsing
in sunny summer rain

Portugal

Three pickpockets
pace the crowded square—
even the pigeons are nervous

Algarve
In the crisp sun in the crag
caverns of the bathwater
heat of low tide, anemones

Paris

Scaffolding on the cathedral—
what is broken
is beyond what they can fix

Norway

Gryf in Hvaler
Storm clouds over pale black rocks
swift a child's early hair
back under a blanket

Skjærhalden
Dense field of black water—
translucent jellyfish
undulant as any voice

Belize

In the TV of my goggles
a stingray folds its smooth fist
over the cock of a nurse shark

An Atlantic of Less Recent Memories

Hellenic Soccer
Stadium ablaze on TV—
islanders whose team has lost celebrate
bottles over each other's skulls

Florence
Red dome, red city—
police block the side streets
& usher fake tourists into a van—
I perfect an interest in gelato

Cannes
Glam—The bronze woman, bored,
Gusto—topless, alone on the beach,
Glitter—is never alone on the beach

Hwy 1 to Loreto
Desert asphalt outpost—
through the car window a young man
pushes red cactus fruit to my lips

US1

Even in Melbourne—
mourning dove at the creek—
I long for Melbourne

A1A

Patrick Air Force Base
The ocean nibbles
a bit more from the dunes—
the rockets remain stoic

Nineteen Years
after My Nineteenth Year

1.

Mayfly
in my coffee, stroking
(goddammit) down my throat

Rickshaw cyclist bows
his legs nicely in a slow
dance up a steep hill

The October moon arrives
with a French manicure,
propositioning stars

The child holding his coat
aloft by one arm is held
aloft by one arm

2.

Bathrobes at our knees sweep
the foyer, a single cherry
tumbles between our tongues

Sawgrass wilting—
bald man on a park bench
popping bubble wrap

Leaves about their feet,
        two blind men
compare dogs

Cigarette butts
        crossing their eyes
in a snowball

3.

Spring rain drums the window—
　　　my refrigerator hums
　　　　　its one tune

Wine cork pop—
breeze lilts a dandelion—
I feel forgotten

Early kumquats
on a slender bough—
quarter-notes of gravity

The snowman
& his creator—
two proud bellies

4.

Spring rain,
& all the books slouching
on their spines

Woman & her dog
                    drink
from the same water bottle

Dappled butterfly
pinned to the tine
of a pitchfork

The cow under dogwood
            is the leather glove
nuzzling away the hoarfrost

5.

Big fly,
          fly!
Bigger rain!

Air conditioner clapping—
          you, cockroach, are the Olympic
champion of shoe dodging!

My hands under
          the cubicle lights.
Autumn? Spring?

Huffing my way
through an acre of snow
& suddenly beach sand

6.

First day of spring!
Sun raking up his clouds.
Everyone wears black.

Two men kissing
among tulips—Midwestern
paparazzi can't help themselves

Enough of this wind,
my god! It's like the sea
all over again!

Lone crow in snow
conspires
to be universal

7.

Dower flower,
half your time on earth
spent staring at grass

My hand grasping
her sleeping foot—
even now

Autumn shower—
tin roof—
my attention crisps

New snow, old snow—
world looks the same
in an oil slick

8.

A day of dilly-dallying
her duodenum—
white blossoms

Little girl with flower
watches me watch her
pick her nose

Outside the hip-hop club
with her still inside, my breath
& the street art peel away in layers

Wine for the bakers—
weed for the bakers—
mistletoe for the bakers' wives

9.

Imagining the baby's
breath—imagining
how it got its name

Punctured basketball
left to weeds—time turns
both counter & worldwise

A flat panel of black fire-
wood carved into
produces white stems

Blinded by snow
the ambulance wails
for what it holds

10.

Rooftop flowers—
a block away,
neighbor waves a hand rake

Chubby man
sweats so much
his toupee slips off

Sailboat on the river
has more sails
with my eyes open

Even those whose flavors
Fortune favors: Winter savors
fresh cadavers.

11.

Magnolia blossoms
don't taste the way
they look they might

A man slaps his face,
pinches his arm—shame's
tutor, the mosquito

Pigtails as horns
on a motorcycle helmet—
each day an opera

Christmas Eve saplings
                    tiptoe
to peek in windows

12.

Sound of a muffled saw—
                    but when I look—
a child smirking in a tree fort

Under July's carapace
cameras turn people
into sociopaths

Fireflies weave in tall grasses—
no, not fireflies
but the eyes of several deer

Socks frozen by puddles—
I drink beer from a glass
like a grownup

13.

A bee staggers
out of a tulip—
I'm off to jury duty

Lady in the yellow hat
　　who looks like a rat
　　　　knows it

Two trees in slow disrobing—
between them a bicycle chain
　　　　smiles wryly

The computer's ambient glow—
neither on nor off, asleep while awake—
5:47 AM. I have no children

14.

Homeless guy with no legs
jerks off in the park—
spring arrives in NYC

Blind girl happily
takes pictures
of the shutter

Woman with the pinwheel
tattoo on your ankle,
where is your breeze?

Bean sprouts & wontons
trolling in hot duck soup—
a glacial evening

15.

First she took to God, then pills—
this year's woodpecker
habits last year's hollowed nest

Amateur tourists
          snapping photos
of shitting dogs in July

Cut harvest worm takes separate paths—moonlight kingdom.

Dead artist's notebook—
nudes, scribbles echoing Brancusi—
help me accept there is but one season—

16.

éfaC otnarepsE—nepO syawlA
—the AA'ers & drunk NYU students
laugh suicidal in the 2 AM cold

An orchid outside a West Village café—
bread & cheese, coffee—women
picking loose flakes of nail polish

Laughing hockey player
wears empty
as a badge

Streaming white finches—
gray moss on a black moon—
a waterfall of earrings—
snow dusts the elderly ice skater

17.

No/ one ever scolds/ the/ spring
snow// for breaking with/ form
¯_(ツ)_/¯

To peel the delicate white
from your brown skin
& roll it into little balls—

Slow fan, apartment window
…
street a harem of cicadas

Even the old dog
                    in snow
still wonders at its breath

18.

Hedge face in scattered blossom—
good things in life impractical
as a Japanese typewriter

This heat
& this haircut
defy limits

Subway heartthrob with hair
the color of a gerbera daisy
sucks the prune from her fingers

Two escalators running
parallel in opposite directions—
New Years Eve

19.

Spring Music, 6th Ave & 3rd St
Handballers' thwacks
a lovely dialogue with wall—
blue ball & come hither

Inky glow of the carousel—
every city is a Seurat
& no city as well

Fat hot rain
so unseasonable
even the cars are fuming

After making love
in our small, hot room
I throw open the window to January

Being & Language
as a Junk Drawer

                    pond
                    frog
                    _____ (wait for it)

Drapery is pacifying.
Latex is electric.
Even skwhoralz without eyes
zip & bump along like squirrels.

                    His words a salty artillery:
                    a goat cheese with ancillary bobs
                    of smug & curdled affectations

First Date
Leffe & Stout. Quarterback sneak.
Nervous itch of a bloody hangnail.
Pell mell & Pall Malls.

Midnight—
& I'm not famous
yet

Careful where you
        fly, fly,
there's a war on

Wandering eye
of the drunk coed
settles on Exit

Don't feel bad for your loss,
aspirin bottle—you empty
like a good parent

Band-Aid caught on a shoe—
I can almost hear
your whimper

Love's language a farrago of mondegreen
borne from stuffs in the junk drawer by the fridge

The Novels of Don DeLillo
Each airport. Every waiting room.
A figure figures a figure or two.
Someone coughs. Someone coughs back.

B-bop is hip-hop for Woodstock
folks. Rock is anemic jazz.
Punk is country with faster dogs.
Ska filches reggae's razzmatazz.

The Video Gamer
Popped Adderall & Provigil—
        in the new light, a face
unknown to the bathroom mirror

Young man strokes
his iPhone, its slender bulk
a suburb of brain

In It
Damn it! Omit. Remit. On it.
Emit. Limit. Cement. Trans-
mit a minute's edit. Exit.

Francis Bacon
Interior: Enough's been said.
Exterior: A bird alights on a plane—
a stray mark, a scream—
beauty arrives at the marketplace

How to Lose Your Shi(r)t at Hold 'em
A.K.
2.2.
A.K.2.A.2.

Korean BBQ, with oranges
arranged in a white bowl—
she finds the rhyme in Stonehenge

White Wail
Magniloquence of an iron lily
tongue-deep in an animal sprung
from the depths of a seaman's imagining

Plane over LaGuardia
A mermaid in a pond of lightning—
loose circuit, equine, nibbler of data—
an idea in a gelatinous brain, concussed

Sundown city—any phrase
placed on this 60' wide billboard
will reinforce class distinctions

F Train

Two women in matching outfits
rub each other's ankles,
agree to disagree

G Train (remix)

She is still a virgin
but it's only
twenty-five to nine

L Train

Just got a cheap-shot five-spot inkblot penny-
whistle bitch-slap heart-attack tattoo like you—
erasure by way of addition

ACE Trains

Language is universal.
Music is universal.
Breathing is pretty important, too.

Toy robot warrior of childhood—
as with any relationship
I asked too much of you—
over-toyed-with—one good
wheel turns you toward me
as your head turns away

<u>Bhutto</u>
The moderate's coffin
    descends a staircase
on a hundred hands

Ohanapecosh—difficult to remember—
O H(os)anna peaco(ck) (gu)sh—
Oh Han (Solo) pec(an) Osh(Kosh B'gosh)

All things
their purpose
in dew time

The more apples I have
now, the less I remember
not having them then

Ant disappears down its hole—
there are many cures
for happiness

NyQuil™ Lucid Fever Lucky
Dream Light Emporium

Sleep inhabits me.
Where did I lay down
that *myself* part?

||

||

I cowers. I is moved
to tears. I flits about
the windows, unable
to get out.

= =

= =

Fever dream—gory wasteland—
my grandmother's wish—sweating
out green tea on the station bench.

||

||

Is that the computer
        or my cat's ghost
    breathing?

Someone calls my name as I turn
        into a boxer's fist—
blood spray on a baby's white jumper.

= =

||

||

Incarnations of the laptop—
on, off, sleep—resurrection
mocks the user.

= =

||

||

Cat, I see what
you're watching,
but it's not there.

||

||

= =

Banana-leaves-windstorm.gif—
how they paddle in open air— = =
ours a river no one steps from.

"Eh? Hen? Conch?—Oh no, hon!"
4-H hen—neon cocoon.   = =
Hench-hen—noon hooch.

                    ||

                    ||

Testing pens for a pleasurable
heft—a branch bearing fruit   = =
or a fruit bearing worms.

          ||

          ||

Folks say the worst shit
possible, yet cringe
to read it lettered on the page.

          ||

          ||

Catfish, carp, & shark
eat shit.   = =
That's a fact, Jack.

Hirst's bifurcated animals
contain no great power save arguing
against the humiliation of death's
finality, with great patience.

                    ||

                    ||

Acetaminophen—Ho, hon!
Dextromethorphan—Conch, h_E-h_E!
Doxylamine—Non-.

Being, in Nothingness—
born into creation language—
my love, here this, here me in this.

                    ||

                    ||

Cigarette smoke
blown through a cold
toothache.

                    ||

                    ||

Writing hiccups
does not mean I'm
incapable of murder.

                    ||

                    ||

Day jobs are endgames.
Culture is mind games. I vote   = =   Office lights, why destroy what
siestas, elevenses, & bankers' hours.   is not you? Why not enjoy
                                          community with shadows?

        || ||
        || ||

Waitress brings our wine   Night office window lit up green—
& the old men turn to watch—   = =   someone, please
O, L.H.O.O.Q.   look down for me—

        ||
        ||

Roommate takes   Drunk off its own heartbeat,
one guy into her bedroom—   = =   stroking clavicle of moon—
another slinks in a chair.   a garden thrush bewitched.

                                                  ||
                                                  ||

Anchor ochre overboard—   *That boy could fall*
orankle stenographite—   = =   *into a barrel of titties*
lamposter, impostulate—   *& come out sucking his thumb.*

        ||
        ||

Sleeps like she's sitting,   Red on yellow, nasty // I love you
one leg crossed over—   = =   fellow; red on black, // I loved you
five toes peek from a blanket.   venom lack // let's love & expire

                                                  ||
                                                  ||

"He was a child of God
much like yourself   = =
perhaps."

               ||

               ||

Roll over, baby.
Do I still feel hot, baby?   = =
Baby, roll over.

Maybe rain, maybe not—
               the heavens
roll over in her sleep.

The pleasures of sweat—
each droplet an advocate
of variety in course—
               unregulated,
               unmediated
               wandering—
bring me
my
sickness

The Dude drops world.
Is just. *Adieu*. Drop world
& jet— & yet—

Notes

The translation of the Issa poem arrives from *The Essential Haiku: Versions of Basho, Buson, and Issa*, edited by Robert Hass.

"She is still a virgin / but it's only / twenty-five to nine" is a slightly modified lyric from the Tom Waits song "Heartattack and Vine."

"He was a child of God / much like yourself / perhaps" arrives from Cormac McCarthy's *Child of God.*

"Midnight— / & I'm not famous / yet" arrives from a short story by Barry Hannah, who borrowed it from Jimmy Buffet.

Acknowledgements

My thanks to my editor, Kate Angus, and to Kimberly Steele and everyone at Augury Books. Special thanks also to Erika Jo Brown for her time and suggestions, and to those who read the book prior to publication and wrote a few lines in my favor: Fred Chappell, Joseph Massey, Heather Morgan, and James Shea. This book is dedicated to my wife, Wendy Millar, but is also for the people who appear in these poems, in one form or another, invented or otherwise.

Publications: The poem beginning "Drunk off its own heartbeat" was published in *The Beloit Review*. Four of the six poems constituting "Southwest" were first published in *Canary*. "Over many springs…" was first published in *Chronogram*. The four poems constituting "6." were published in *The Cortland Review*. Each of the poems in the cluster "South Africa" were first published in *Leveler*.

About the Author

Joe Pan is the author of two collections of poetry, *Hiccups* (Augury Books) and *Autobiomythography & Gallery* (BAP). He is the publisher and managing editor of Brooklyn Arts Press, serves as the poetry editor for the arts magazine *Hyperallergic* and as small press editor for *Boog City*, and is the founder of the services-oriented activist group Brooklyn Artists Helping. His piece "Ode to the MQ-9 Reaper," a hybrid work about drones, was excerpted and praised in *The New York Times*. In 2015 Joe participated in the Lower Manhattan Cultural Council's Process Space artist residency program on Governors Island. Joe attended the Iowa Writers' Workshop, grew up along the Space Coast of Florida, and now lives in Williamsburg, Brooklyn.